Make Happy Choices

High Hopes Publishing

ISBN 978-0-9905129-0-5

Cover designed by David Ellsworth

High Hopes Publishing
Georgetown, TX
(512) 868-0548
www.highhopespublishing.com

This Book is a Gift for:

_____

Message:

_____

_____

_____

_____

_____

From:

_____

Disclaimer

The purpose of this book is to educate and entertain. The material contained herein is not intended to be a substitute for the advice of your mentors. We encourage the reader to regularly consult with a financial advisor or other coach with respect to any topics presented herein.

This book is sold with the understanding that the publisher/author is not able to provide information on your specific circumstances. You are encouraged to read all available material, learn as much as possible, and tailor the information to your individual needs.

The author, publisher, or anyone included in this book shall have no liability or responsibility to any person or entity with respect to any loss or damage caused or alleged to have been caused directly or indirectly by the information contained in this book.

The names of some individuals and identifying details may have been changed to protect the privacy of those individuals.

Reflect . . .

Unlearn . . .

Live Better. . .

--William Teh

Dedication

To my loving wife Sandra, and children Nathan and Hannah:

My wish is to let you know that you are the reason for my happiness, and for us to live, and share a joyful life together by making happy choices.

To Nathan and Hannah, my wish is to leave this book of choices for you, and to share some of Papa's thoughts about how happiness can be a choice for you.
Most importantly, I want to let you know that Papa and Mama love you more than anything else in the whole, wide world.

Love you forever,

Papa Teh

Table of Contents

Acknowledgement

I wish to thank everyone who has made an impact, left an impression, or been an influence in my life. The lessons unlearned, learning experiences, and impressions made, helped make the chapters come across with a little more "Sizzle and Pop".

In an effort to draft *Make Happy Choices* as a short and simple read, I have only captured some of my more impactful experiences in this book. I humbly beg the understanding of my family, friends, and business partners whose stories I have failed to fully discuss or mention.

Last and not least, I wish to thank my dear friend, editor and publisher Gene Vasconi for the thoughtful care, insightful advice, and quality of time he has spent together with me in preparing *Make Happy Choices* to share with you.

Foreword

I first met William when I was conducting a workshop on investing retirement money. He stood out in the group because, not only did he have a full head of hair - none of it was grey. When the session ended, the group filed out; however William remained seated. He introduced himself, was very respectful, asked several great questions, and I was impressed.

I thought to myself, "he is a young man, but at least 10-20 years ahead of his peers in the way he thinks". My feelings were reinforced when I read his first book, "13 Ways to Accomplish More by Doing Less".

William has built on his earlier book with this one, "Make Happy Choices". Don't let the title deceive you; it is a profound book with a terrific message.

William has written a book about basic values. To be happy you must have a good set of core values and principles as a foundation for happiness. Happy Choices does not mean going down the road of least resistance; but rather making right choices because you have a better understanding about life and your values.

William's writing style is such that this is a multi-generational book. It can be read and understood by all. If you are a child getting started, a parent, teacher, coach or grandparent turned mentor, there is something in this book for you. This is not just a book to be read over the course of an evening. It is a terrific instrument for understanding and teaching many of the basic values in life. The chapter tools will enhance your life and serve as a vehicle for you to pass down some good principles from generation to generation.

Dennis Miller
Editor of Miller's Money Forever
A Casey Research Publication
www.Millersmoney.com

Introduction:

This book is a collection of a dozen simple and overlooked concepts, ideas, and strategies hidden in broad daylight that I discovered to help me better understand and make happier choices.

For some of us, happiness is an elusive state. I believe a path to happiness can begin by making happy choices. I believe that making choices to achieve perfection or to satisfy desires is not the same as making happy choices. I also believe that it is more difficult to be happy constantly hanging around negative people.

It seems obvious that everyone should know how to make happy choices. However, if that were so, we would know lots of happy people who are living their happy choices, and happy to share them with us.

I am grateful for all my learning experiences, life's lessons, and mostly to my family, friends, and business partners who offer me refreshing new perspectives on making happy choices, and having an appreciative outlook on life.

By reframing how I think, redesigning how I make choices, and choosing the right people who surround me, I am greatly able to influence the quality and happiness of my life.

Writing this book has been one of my happiest choices. Thank you for providing me the opportunity to share with you some of my limiting beliefs, misplaced priorities, and "Ah Hah!" moments that I discovered along the way.

I look forward to visiting with you again at the end of the book.

Please enjoy.

William Teh

Chapter 1
Choose to be Rich or Poor

Being Rich and Poor can be measured
We can use the 2014 US Income Tax Brackets and Rates as a simple way to measure if we are rich or poor. This is probably the most common and widely accepted way to determine if you are rich or poor.

Here is the table for the Lowest and Highest Income Tax Filers:

Rate	Single	Married Joint	Head of Household
10.0%	$0 to $9,075	$0 to $18,150	$0 to $12,950
39.6%	$406,751+	$457,601+	$432,201+

Source: Internal Revenue Service

So, if we use the income tax bracket as a metric for measuring wealth, the taxing government/entity can infer if we are rich or poor.

More importantly, being Rich or Poor may also be more a matter of choice than chance. Why can we say that? Well, let's try working through this simple exercise...

- If we consistently make a series of good, smart, or prudent choices, we will most likely be Rich.

- If we consistently make a series of poor, uninformed, irresponsible choices, we will most likely be Poor.

- Therefore, if we understand, believe, and agree with this reasoning, simply stated being Rich or Poor is a choice.

What is the definition of Money?

What is the definition of Money? I suggest that Money represents having choices. The more money we have, the more choices we have. The less money we have, the fewer choices we have.

Just for a moment, let's think about having money as a bank account of choices instead of dollars. When we reframe our thoughts about money as choices, perhaps we will also have to be mindful that we will need to be in good spirits, have good health, and free time to wisely consume, share, or gift away our choices.

Being Rich can be as simple as making it a Habit

Let's break this down a little more. So what do we call making a series of consistent choices? I suggest that making a series of consistent choices is called a HABIT.

Wait a minute! So to be Rich or Poor could be as simple as cultivating Rich or Poor HABITS? Yup.

Allow me to share with you "The 10 Habits of Self-Made Millionaires" compiled by David Weiver, and my take on them...

1. **Millionaires are Frugal**
   "Buy Income Producing Assets. When your passive income is greater than your expenses, you can live your purpose and desired lifestyle without worrying about running out of money."

2. **Millionaires Think BIG**
   "The bigger your dream, vision, or goals to help other people, the better quality of people you can attract to build your team."

3. **Millionaires Take Calculated Risks**
   "Calculate your Best Case, Most Likely, and Worst Case outcome for your investments. If you are willing to risk accepting the WORST CASE outcome for a chance at achieving your BEST CASE outcome -- Do It."

4. **Millionaires Network**
   "Your Net-work equals your Net-worth."

5. **Millionaires Don't Pay Interest, They Earn It**
"Don't work for money. Make your money work for you. Work to learn."

6. **Millionaires are Focused**
"A Focused mind accomplishes more than the monkey mind."

7. **Millionaires Do Whatever It Takes**
"Never give up on your Purpose."

8. **Millionaires Educate Themselves**
"Stay current, relevant, and forward looking."

9. **Millionaires Lead**
"Sustainable Leadership is Invisible Leadership."

10. **Millionaires Are Generous**
"Being generous is nice, builds trust, and shows leadership."

Quotes:

- "Being the richest man in the cemetery doesn't matter to me." Steve Jobs

- "Nobody became Rich or Poor... Alone." William Teh

- "Learn. Earn. Give Back." Dr. Nido Qubein

- "Nothing is work unless you'd rather be doing something else." George Halas

Summary:

- Being Rich or Poor is a Choice

- Consistent Choices = Habit

- Cultivate Wealthy Habits

Chapter 1: Happy Choices 5 Minute Review

1. What are your 3 main takeaways?

   i_____

   ii_____

   iii_____

2. Are you Happy with your present Situation? YES/NO

3. If YES: What are the 3 things you can do more to improve?

   i_____

   ii_____

   iii_____

4. If NO: Reflect on 3 things that you are unhappy with:

   i_____

   ii_____

   iii_____

5. What are 3 things you can unlearn to be less unhappy/more Happy?

   i_____

   ii_____

   iii_____

Chapter 2
Choose to be Cheap or Generous

We do not need money to be Cheap or Generous. I believe being Cheap or Generous is more of a mindset, attitude, and may be also be a result of our past experiences.

When we come from a place of want, a mindset of scarcity, or experience that people are generally not nice, we may tend to be cheap.

If we come from a mindset of abundance, or think that people are generally nice, we may tend to be more generous.

"We act according to what we believe and feel."

Sometimes people confuse the idea that to be generous, we need to have money. I would suggest that we can also be generous with our time or energy, and it may have a greater influential impact.

It is not the amount of time or energy that we offer that makes us generous, but rather the quality. The quality of time and energy that we offer is best measured by the impact on the person(s) receiving our time and energy. I believe that desirable impact is directly proportional to the level of needed or quality of attention received.

I would exercise prudence when sharing our time, energy or money. As my mentor Dr. Nido Qubein so elegantly summarizes it, "Be selectively extravagant, and prudently frugal."

Quotes:

- "With a bucket of water, we can choose to water a plant, or a thousand weeds." William Teh

- "Not everything that can be counted counts . . . and not everything that counts can be counted." Albert Einstein

- "There are people who have money and people who are rich." Coco Chanel

Summary:

- Being Cheap or Generous is a Mindset

- We can accomplish more by being generous

Chapter 2: Happy Choices 5 Minute Review

1. What are your 3 main takeaways?

    i_____

    ii_____

    iii_____

2. Are you Happy with your present Situation?   YES/NO?

3. If YES: What are the 3 things you can do more to improve?

    i_____

    ii_____

    iii_____

4. If NO: Reflect on 3 things that you are unhappy with:

    i_____

    ii_____

    iii_____

5. What are 3 things you can unlearn to be less unhappy/more Happy?

    i_____

    ii_____

    iii_____

Chapter 3
Choose to invest for
Financial Security or Financial Freedom

If information were power, anyone who has access to the Internet would be a millionaire, have 6-pack abs, look gorgeous and . . . live happily ever after.

Preparing for Financial Security
Direct and live from the Internet, here are the top 10 ways to prepare for retirement as suggested by the United States Department of Labor:

1. Start saving, keep saving, and stick to your goals

2. Know your retirement needs

3. Contribute to your employer's retirement savings plan

4. Learn about your employer's pension plan

5. Consider basic investment principles

6. Don't touch your retirement savings

7. Ask your employer to start a plan

8. Put money into an individual retirement account

9. Find out about your Social Security benefits

10. Ask questions

These are 10 Great "Retirement" tips as suggested by the "Highest" authority.

Financial Security planning seems at best to create a plan to help us survive through our retirement years. Unfortunately, I believe there are at least three simple assumptions that are not being considered . . .

Assumption #1:
What if I don't live long enough to retire?

Assumption #2:
What if the retirement tax laws change?

Assumption #3:
What can I do to start living well today till I expire?

Perhaps the greatest assumption may be that the 40-40-40 Financial Security plan is not for everyone.

What is the 40-40-40 plan?
Work 40 hours a week for the next 40 years, and retire on 40% of your income.

This is my understanding of Financial Security as taught by mainstream financial advisers, and the United States Department of Labor:

- Live with the belief that wealth is finite

- Live below our means

- Live with a mindset of scarcity

Mother Goose has a great nursery rhyme that, in a half dozen lyrics, captures the shortcomings for investing for financial security, or building your nest egg for retirement.

> *Old Mother Hubbard*
> *Went to the cupboard*
> *To get her poor dog a bone;*
> *But when she got there*
> *The cupboard was bare,*
> *And so the poor dog had none.*

This is the best financial security plan that I've heard:

> *"The last check we write to the undertaker should bounce."*

Investing for Financial Freedom
The definition of Financial Independence or Freedom by Wikipedia is:

"Financial Independence is generally used to describe the state of having sufficient personal wealth to live, without having to work actively for basic necessities. For financially independent people, their assets generate income that is greater than their expenses."

The goal to achieve Financial Freedom or Independence sounds like a much better plan to me than to prepare for Financial Security.

My understanding of Financial Freedom is:

"...having the ability to do what we want, with whom we want, whenever we want, without ever worrying about running out of money."

Definition of Financially wealthy people
I love Gary Keller's definition of financially wealthy people: "Someone who has enough money coming in without having to work to finance their purpose in life."

When we design our businesses to generate a Passive Cash flow greater than our monthly expenses, we will be free from needing to work for a paycheck.

What type of millionaire do you want to be?
A Net Worth Millionaire or Cash Flow Millionaire?

Quotes:

- "I have observed that men give up their health to make a lot of money. After they have acquired a lot of money, they spend their money to get back their health." Dali Lama.

- "Information is not power." William Teh

- "Invest to achieve your desired lifestyle." William Teh

- "It is neither wealth nor splendor; but tranquility and occupation which give you happiness." Thomas Jefferson

- "Our freedom can be measured by the number of things we can walk away from." Vernon Howard

Summary:

- Invest for Financial Freedom = Passive Cash Flow

- Passive Cash Flow (creates) Lifestyle (creates) Happiness

Chapter 3: Happy Choices 5 Minute Review

1. What are your 3 main takeaways?

   i_____

   ii_____

   iii_____

2. Are you Happy with your present Situation?   YES/NO

3. If YES: What are the 3 things you can do more to improve?

   i_____

   ii_____

   iii_____

4. If NO: Reflect on 3 things that you are unhappy with:

   i_____

   ii_____

   iii_____

5. What are 3 things you can unlearn to be less unhappy/more Happy?

   i_____

   ii_____

   iii_____

Chapter 4
Choose Happiness as a Destination or Journey

Have you heard the song sung by Kenny Chesney "Everybody wants to go to heaven"? The key theme of the song is in this sentence: "Everybody wants to go to heaven, but nobody wants to go now."

We may have observed that some folks just exist or get by, and seem to hope to go to a better place after they expire.

Sentimental People
The definition of "Sentimental" is feelings of tenderness, sadness, or nostalgia.

I believe sentimental people tend to:
- Remember the past better or worse than it was
- Accumulate memories and possessions from the past
- Generally feel blue

Romantic People
The definition of "Romantic" is being inclined toward a suggestive feeling of excitement and mystery associated with love; characterized by (or suggestive of) an idealized view of reality.

I believe romantic people tend to:
- Live for today
- Dream and prepare for a better tomorrow
- Generally be happy

In summary, I think Romantic people tend to be more appreciative, live life larger, and are happier.

It is easier to be romantic when we have more free time, good health, and money to do the things we like with the people we want.

Wait a minute! Doesn't being romantic sound strangely familiar . . . like having Financial Freedom?

I believe investing for Financial Freedom to generate an infinite stream of passive income is a better way to create more free time to be romantic.

Quotes:

- "10 years ago we had Steve Jobs, Bob Hope, and Johnny Cash. Today, we have no Jobs, no Hope, and no Cash."Unknown

- "The more clutter we introduce into our lives, the more elusive happiness becomes." William Teh

- "Cash Flow is Sexy." David Lindahl

Summary:

- If we do it right, we can enjoy both the journey and destination to be happy

- Build and Keep an Inventory of Free Time, Money, and Health

- Financial Freedom creates Romance

Chapter 4: Happy Choices 5 Minute Review

1. What are your 3 main takeaways?

     i_____

     ii_____

     iii_____

2. Are you Happy with your present Situation?   YES/NO

3. If YES: What are the 3 things you can do more to improve?

     i_____

     ii_____

     iii_____

4. If NO: Reflect on 3 things that you are unhappy with:

     i_____

     ii_____

     iii_____

5. What are 3 things you can unlearn to be less unhappy/more Happy?

     i_____

     ii_____

     iii_____

Chapter 5
Choose to Shop for Price or Pay for Value

"Price is what we pay. Value is what we get."
Warren Buffett.

Folks who shop for Price generally think about purchases as either Cheap or Expensive.

Folks who shop for Value generally think about purchases as being either of Good Value or Poor Value.

What is Value?
What is the definition of value? According to the Oxford Dictionary, value is defined as, "The regard that something is held to deserve, the importance, worth, or usefulness of something."

For something we buy, the clearer we are with the benefits derived from the purchase, the more definite we can establish its value.

Value from Doing Business or Investing
In doing business, I would define value as, "What will someone pay me to buy what I am offering?"

For a product offering, when the market will compensate us more than our cost of acquisition, the product has positive value to us. Otherwise the product will have Zero or Negative value to us.

For a service offering, when the market will compensate us more to perform that service than to do something else, then performing that service is the Highest and Best use of our time. Otherwise, find something else to do.

Our business goal is to establish, understand, and educate our customers of the higher value they will enjoy by making the transaction with us.

A transaction will occur when both the Buyer, and Seller feel that that the value received is greater than the value given up (e.g. Product, Service, or Money.)

Compensation can be in the form of Financial Capital, Relationship Capital, or Educational Capital. We will discuss these three types of Capital in the next chapter.

When investing, it may be more profitable, safer and prudent to always begin with the end in mind. It may be a good idea to begin by considering multiple exit strategies before acquiring the supposed asset.

In a free market, the consumer or customer ALWAYS determines value of the transaction.

Value of a Business Relationship

My opinion of value for a business relationship is this . . . "The value of a relationship is directly related to the size of the problem that they can solve for me."

Quotes:
- "We should seek the greatest value of our action." Stephen Hawking

- "Simplicity in character, in manners, in style; in all things the supreme excellence is simplicity." Henry Wadsworth Longfellow

- "Results count. Everything else is style." William Teh

Summary:
- The more clearly we identify the benefits of a purchase; the more clearly we establish the value of the purchase.

- When investing, before you buy, think about what you can sell the investment for. Begin with the end in mind.

- Value of a Business Relationship: "The bigger the problem you can solve for me, the more valuable is the relationship."

Chapter 5: Happy Choices 5 Minute Review

1. What are your 3 main takeaways?

    i_____

    ii_____

    iii_____

2. Are you Happy with your present Situation?   YES/NO

3. If YES: What are the 3 things you can do more to improve?

    i_____

    ii_____

    iii_____

4. If NO: Reflect on 3 things that you are unhappy with:

    i_____

    ii_____

    iii_____

    What are 3 things you can unlearn to be less unhappy/more Happy?

    i_____

    ii_____

    iii_____

Chapter 6
Choose to invest for Money
or in Relationships

In the first chapter, we discussed that Money represents Choices. If we make good or poor choices, we will have either more or less choices (Money).

I believe that to create, enjoy, and have more choices, we may wish to consider investing in mutually productive relationships.

Dr. Nido Qubin teaches the three keys to building a productive relationship and my take on them:

Know:
"We begin a relationship by first getting to know the person so that we can establish lines of communication. Getting an introduction or referral can "short cycle" finding the right people to connect."

Like:
"A relationship will develop when we like each other enough to start building bridges of understanding."

Trust:
"When trust is mutually earned, it can be monetized by making an investment of time, energy, or money together."

Regardless of the purpose of the relationship, with family, friends, or for business, it may be prudent to be mindful of these 3 simple relationship-building steps. The relationship is tested when difficult times arise.

To further expand on the discussion of establishing a productive business relationship, I learned through experience that it is prudent to check for these 3 attributes:

Skills check:
Do our partners bring complementary skills and relationships to the table to accelerate, grow, or open new doors for our business?

Attitude Adjustment:
Do our partners have the right attitude and personality for the roles they are assuming in the business?

Values Clarification:
If we partnered with a person that has great skills, and attitude, but with incongruent values, I believe that relationship is unsustainable, and may eventually become non-productive or worse

yet, destructive. Values are tested when difficult times arise.

Values clarification is THE most important attribute of a business relationship. Our values drive all if not most of the decisions for seizing opportunities, mitigating risks, and managing expectations.

What type of Capital are we accumulating?
I would suggest that there are three types of Capital we ought to accumulate:

Financial Capital
We accumulate Financial Capital in our pockets

Educational Capital
We accumulate Educational Capital between our ears

Relationship Capital
We accumulate Relationship Capital in the hearts of our fans, friends, and family.

Applying the Sustainability Test to Accumulating Capital
In my earlier book "13 Ways to Accomplish More by Doing Less" we discussed how we understood Success, and Significance. Here is a quick recap.

What is Success?
Success is what we achieve.

What is Significance?
Significance is what we help other people achieve.

May I recommend applying the sustainability test when accumulating our capital? The sustainability test consists of the Significance, Success, and Stress tests:

Sustainability Tests for Accumulating Financial Capital
Significance Test:
Who are we helping as we accumulate our Financial Capital?

Success Test:
What is the Return on Investment on our Financial Capital?
Are we financially better today than yesterday?

Stress Test:
Who will help us when we lose or cannot manage our financial capital?

Sustainability Tests for Accumulating Educational Capital

Significance Test:
Who are we helping as we accumulate our Educational Capital?

Success Test:
What is the Return on Investment on our Educational Capital?
Are we able to make better choices with less information in less time?

Stress Test:
Who will help us avoid making poor choices, or help us when we have made a poor choice?

Sustainability Tests for Accumulating Relationship Capital

Significance Test:
To whom are we a positive influence in their lives?

Success Test:
What is the Return on Investment on our Relational Capital?
Are we spending more quality time with people we Know, Like and Trust?

Stress Test:
Who will help in us in our time of need?

Impact of the Sustainability Test:
The sustainability test can provide either a "Whatever", "Ah Hah!" or "OMG!" response for us.

Now may be an excellent time to take a recess to reassess how we spend our time, energy, and efforts. We can re-examine our beliefs, reframe our thoughts, or refocus our priorities to accumulate the 3 types of capital in a more sustainable way.

I would further suggest that the answers we offer for the Significance Test questions directly impact the responses we come up with for the Stress Test questions.

Conversation with Jim Stehlik at Rudy's BBQ:
Back in 2008, Jim Stehlik and I connected at a "Rich Dad" Real Estate event. Jim was one of the coaching mentors, and I was a student. I chatted with most of the subject matter coaches at the event while interviewing the coaches. After chatting with the coaches, I felt that I had the best connection with Jim, and I picked him for my 3-day on-site training. To-date, Jim still coaches me personally, and we have also become great friends along the way.

Jim is an amazing person. He will put guys half his age to shame with the amount of energy, drive, and dedication he has for his family, work, and music. Jim travels the country helping people get started in their real estate investments by mentoring them one-on-one. He has helped over 400 people. Today, Jim is much more selective about whom he spends time with and coaches. When he is not working, Jim spends every free moment and more with his wife and three children, of which the youngest two are twins. Jim is also an accomplished pianist of more than 35 years.

Back in April of 2014, Jim spontaneously reached out to me to let me know that he had an opportunity to come pay me a visit in Austin, TX before meeting his client. It was on short notice, and I am always mindful to make the time we spend together engaging, meaningful, and productive for both of us.

We wound up Jim's visit to Austin by going for an early dinner at Rudy's BBQ store before I dropped him off at the airport to catch his next flight to Dallas, TX. We picked the Rudy's store on South Capital of TX highway.

Max Aue founded Rudy's in 1800's. Rudy's started out as a one-stop gas station, garage, and grocery store in the small community of Leon Springs, just north of San Antonio, TX. Barbeque was added to the operation in 1989, and Rudy's "Country Store" has been serving up tasty Bar-B-Q ever since.

We ordered St. Louis Ribs, Baby Back Ribs, extra moist Brisket, and some delicious cream corn. The weather was great, so we sat outside in the back to enjoy our meal in the great spring weather.

We chatted about material ranging from investing, market trends, forming strategic alliances, and cultivating business relationships. As we chatted about the topic of why some people just seem to always be "lucky" and others always seem to "struggle" with forming great relationships, Jim shared this story with me of how, in the big picture scheme of things, people will reflect what we are.

Moving into Town

Once there was an out-of-town couple looking to move into town and wanted to learn more about the type of people who lived here. They approached and asked the mayor of the town, "Mayor, what kinds of people live here? Are the people who live here nice?" Mayor smiles back, and asks them a question, "In the town where you came from, were the people nice?" The couple answered, "We moved out of our old town because the people were not nice. They were unfriendly, impolite, and unhelpful."

"Well" said the mayor, "I'm sorry, you'll find the same kind of people here too." The couple was very sad to hear the mayor's feedback, and decided to move on and find a better town to live in.

The next day, another out-of-town couple looking to move into town came to visit the mayor. They asked the mayor of the town: "Mayor, are the people who live here nice?" Mayor smiles back and asks them the same question: "In the town you came from, were the people nice?" The couple answered, "Yes! The people were very nice. They were friendly, courteous, always willing to lend a helping hand."

"Well" said the mayor, "Welcome to my town, you'll find the same kind of people here too." The family was glad to hear the mayor's feedback, they moved into town, and settled in happily.

Quotes:
- "A true friend never gets in your way unless you happen to be going down." Arnold H. Glasowf

- "Rich People invest in Assets. Wealthy People invest in Relationships." William Teh

- "You can't schedule opportunity." William Teh

- "Doing business is just an excuse to eat lunch together." William Teh

- "Be smart and you take care of yourself. Be prudent and take care of your smart friends who will look after you." William Teh

Summary:

- Know. Like. Trust. Follow these steps to build relationships.

- Check for Complementary Skills, Attitudes, and Common Values when forming business relationships.

- Accumulate Financial, Educational, and Relationship Capital in a sustainable way.

Chapter 6: Happy Choices 5 Minute Review

1. What are your 3 main takeaways?

    i_____

    ii_____

    iii_____

2. Are you Happy with your present Situation?   YES/NO

3. If YES: What are the 3 things you can do more to improve?

    i_____

    ii_____

    iii_____

4. If NO: Reflect on 3 things that you are unhappy with:

    i_____

    ii_____

    iii_____

5. What are 3 things you can unlearn to be less unhappy/more Happy?

    i_____

    ii_____

    iii_____

Chapter 7
Choose to Seek
Perfection or Excellence

Have you ever seen the perfect sunset? Experienced the perfect vacation? Wore the perfect suit or dress? Guess what? 20 minutes later, the perfect sunset is gone. The perfect vacation comes to an end when you pack up to go home. 10 years later and some 15 pounds heavier, the perfect suit or dress no longer fits comfortably.

When we focus on having the perfect outcome, we will probably have a very high probability of feeling disappointed, angry, or frustrated when the preparation, process or outcome is less than perfect. Sounds like a perfect way to create an unhappy ending.

When we focus on encouraging, bringing out the best in people, and being able to laugh at our blunders, it makes everyone want to do better and takes away negative stress. Sounds like an excellent way to design a happy journey.

Perfection:
According to the Oxford Dictionary, the definition of perfection is, "the condition, state or quality of being free or as free as possible from all flaws or defects."

I believe that Perfection is an opinion. Maintaining Perfection is **non-sustainable**, as conditions, opinions, and times constantly change. Any deviation from perfection may cause stress and unhappiness to a perfectionist.

Excellence:
According the Oxford Dictionary, the definition of excellence is, "the quality of being outstanding or extremely good."

I believe that Excellence is a standard. Maintaining Excellence **is sustainable**. Any deviation from excellence is an opportunity to improve.

In businesses, I do not know who has the perfect business system. But I am sure most of us can recognize an excellent business system. It is one that is continuously evolving, improving their service level and providing desirable products to meet or exceed the needs of their chosen markets.

In life or in business, if we are not getting ahead or better, we are falling behind.

Getting coaching is a great way to achieve, and sustain excellence. When the time is right, we can continue to evolve and contribute by coaching on the subject matter we have excelled in.

Depending on our goal to be perfect or excellent, it can either be a happy or unhappy experience for us and/or our support team.

The Cracked Pot

Please enjoy the story of the cracked pot, where a less than perfect pot may be able to create more value than a perfect pot.

The Cracked Pot
By Sacinandana Swami

A water bearer in India had two large pots, each hung on one end of the pole he carried across the back of his neck. One of the pots had a crack in it and, while the other pot was perfect and always delivered a full portion of water at the end of the long walk from the stream, the cracked pot arrived only half full. This went on every day for two years, with the bearer delivering only one and a half pots of water to his master's house.

Of course, the perfect pot was proud of its accomplishment and saw itself as perfectly suited for the purpose for which it was made. But the poor cracked pot was ashamed of its imperfection and miserable that it was able to accomplish only half of what it had been made to do. After two years of what it perceived as bitter failure, it spoke to the water bearer one day by the stream. "I am ashamed of myself and I want to apologize to you."

"Why?" asked the bearer. "What are you ashamed of?"

"For the past two years, I have been able to deliver only half my load because this crack in my side causes water to leak out all the way back to your master's house. Because of my flaws you have to work without getting the full value of your efforts," the pot said.

The water bearer felt sorry for the old cracked pot, and out of compassion he said, "As we return to the master's house, I want you to notice the beautiful flowers along the path." Indeed, as they went up the hill, the old cracked pot took notice of the sun warming the wildflowers on the side of the path. The pot felt cheered.

But at the end of the trail, the pot still felt bad because it had leaked out half its load, and again it apologized for its failure. The bearer said to the pot, "Did you notice that there were flowers only on your side of your path, but not on the other pot's side? That's because I knew about your flaw and took advantage of it. I planted flower seeds on your side of the path, and every day while we walk back from the stream, you've watered them for me. For two years I have been able to pick these beautiful flowers to decorate my master's table. If you were not just the way you are, he would not have such beauty to grace his house.

Quotes:

- "The greatest mistake you can make in life is to continually fear you will make one." Elbert Hubbard

- "Do your best, and I will take care of the rest." Chief Master Michael Niblock, 9th Degree Black Belt Tai Kwon Do instructor

- "If the world were perfect, it wouldn't be." Yogi Berra

- "Excellence is a standard. Perfection is an opinion." William Teh

- "We are not born perfect. We are born special." William Teh

Summary:

- Perfection ends when there is a change.

- Excellence is continuous improvement.

Chapter 7: Happy Choices 5 Minute Review

1. What are your 3 main takeaways?

   i_____

   ii_____

   iii_____

2. Are you Happy with your present Situation?   YES/NO

3. If YES: What are the 3 things you can do more to improve?

   i_____

   ii_____

   iii_____

4. If NO: Reflect on 3 things that you are unhappy with:

   i_____

   ii_____

   iii_____

5. What are 3 things you can unlearn to be less unhappy/more Happy?

   i_____

   ii_____

   iii_____

Chapter 8
Choose to Find a Better Answer
or Ask a Better Question

When we moved Austin, TX, my wife Sandra did a lot of research before finding the right school for our children. The focus was on inquiry-based learning and engagement, which I understood as encouraging students to learn by asking questions, and enjoy the learning process. The school encourages students to believe in their own talents and take ownership of their own unique paths of learning.

It appears that designing a program to learn by asking questions, accelerates the mind to think more creatively, critically, and constructively.

In the last couple of years, my wife Sandra introduced and connected me with Reynaldy. Two years ago (2012) Reynaldy came to Austin from Indonesia to pursue his Ph. D. in Geology. A year later, his wife Desi, and one year old daughter Sasya came over to join him and complete the family. Since then, we have become great friends.

I find great insights when I listen to Reynaldy talk about his work, field experiences, and working for a highly successful Ph. D. geologist educator, businessman, and entrepreneur.

I'd like to compile, summarize and embellish what I learned from listening to Reynaldy and apply the principles over to investing into 7 simple steps:

1. Objectively define the Purpose of your Mission, and then set your Goals.

2. The more knowledgeable you are with the subject matter, the better the quality of questions you can ask to clarify and set your goals.

3. Design, define, and sequence the tasks to achieve your goals.

4. Identify your non-delegable tasks, and delegate the rest.

5. Take responsibility for all mistakes, shortcomings, and failures.

6. * Be Generous. Compensate your team well for performance. Give credit to your team who worked for you.

   *Here is where you can monetize being generous!

7. If accomplishing the goal brought you closer to your purpose, set another goal, and repeat the process.

It would seem that the quality of the answer given is directly proportional to the quality of the question asked.

Three Question Test for Success
The answers we give to these three questions may provide some enlightenment about where we currently are and where we may be heading.
(There are no right or wrong answers)

Who are 5 people you spend the most time with?

- Our net worth is usually the average of the 5 people we hang around with.

- Sometimes to get ahead it is not so important what we know or whom we know, but rather who knows us.

- The type of relationship we have will determine what we will do for them, and more importantly what they will do for us.

What do you do in your free time?
- How we spend our free time will usually determine if we are staying current, relevant, or becoming irrelevant.

- What we do in our free time is a good indicator of what we enjoy doing. Now, if we can harmonize what we enjoy doing with making money, then the four letter word "W-O-R-K" becomes irrelevant. Monetize your playtime.

- Who we spend our free time with may also influence our ability to get ahead, stay the same, or hold us back.

What type of books do you read?
- What and whom we read is a good indicator of what we feed our mind.

- Some people say we are what we eat. We can extend that to also say, we are what we read.

- Some of us gladly spend money and time to take vacations, eat out, or attend sporting events, but don't have the time or money to buy a good book to read.

According to the United Stated Bureau of Labor Statistics, from year 2000 to 2008, this is what the average family spent for entertainment and reading in a year:

Item	Dollars	% Household Income
Entertainment	$2,827	5.6%
Reading	$ 101	0.2%

If I calculate correctly, we spend about 28 times more money on Entertainment than on Reading.

Quotes:

- "We would pay more for entertainment than we would for education." Johnny Carson

- "Honest disagreement is often a good sign of progress." Mahatma Gandhi

- "Our main business is not to see what lies dimly at a distance, but to do what lies clearly at hand." Thomas Carlyle.

- "Progress begins by asking a better question." William Teh

Summary:

- Progress begins by asking a better question.

Chapter 8: Happy Choices 5 Minute Review

1. What are your 3 main takeaways?

   i_____

   ii_____

   iii_____

2. Are you Happy with your present Situation?   YES/NO

3. If YES: What are the 3 things you can do more to improve?

   i_____

   ii_____

   iii_____

4. If NO: Reflect on 3 things that you are unhappy with:

   i_____

   ii_____

   iii_____

5. What are 3 things you can unlearn to be less unhappy/more Happy?

   i_____

   ii_____

   iii_____

Chapter 9
Choose to Do Everything
or Your One Thing

Back on May 15, 2013 on a Wednesday evening, my wife Sandra and I went out on our first couples' date with our good friends Tony and his wife Hani. Since Nathan and Hannah were born, the children have always been with at least one of us. So this was a BIG event for us.

Planning to leave Nathan and Hannah alone for a couple of hours for an evening was a big project. Sandra was not comfortable leaving the children with just any babysitter and called on her good friend Yuni to see if she would have time to come to our home to babysit for a couple of hours after work. Yuni was very kind and generous. She told us to go have an evening out, and to always remember to make a little time for ourselves as a couple. Yuni works very hard and has a daughter of her own, so she was giving us some advice from a position of experience.

Aunty Yuni came to our home around 6:30p.m. and Sandra was nervous, especially for Hannah. Aunty Yuni assured us that everything would be OK, and that's what cell phones were for.

We packed up and left to go see a live El Divo concert at the Moody Theater.

El Divo is a cosmopolitan quartet of pop/opera crossover singers made up of four singers created by the music manager Simon Cowell. Simon Cowell is probably most well known in the United States for his role as talent judge on "American Idol".

Music manager Simon Cowell had the vision to create El Divo. The singers prior to forming El Divo were each successful by themselves, but together as the quartet, they broke and made records.

The El Divo quartet is made up of the French pop singer SébastienIzambard, American tenor David Miller, Swiss tenor UrsBühler, and Spanish Baritone Carlos Marín. Together as El Divo, they sing in Spanish, English, Italian, French, and Latin.

El Divo was named the "Most Multinational UK No. 1 Album Group" in the 2006 edition of the Guinness Book of World Records. To date, they have sold more than 26 million albums worldwide.

Together, you can accomplish so much more, while still singing your own tune.

Wow. We really had a good time and enjoyed the concert. It is so different to listen to a live concert than watching them sing on TV. The energy, the ambiance, and just being totally immersed into the experience cannot be replicated unless one is there.

Although the concert ended way too soon for us, we were anxious to go home to see Nathan and Hannah. Crazy thoughts ran through our minds. What if Hannah was crying because she missed Mama so much? What if Nathan was misbehaving and was giving Aunty Yuni a headache?

Guess what? When we got home, both children were asleep together in our bedroom. Yuni was reading a book in the living room waiting for us. She said Nathan and Hannah were lovely and well behaved children, and that it was a pleasure to spend time with them. We had nothing to worry about.

Order Qualifying Criteria or Order Winning Criteria
When I was in college at the University of Wisconsin-Whitewater working on getting a degree in Business, my professor for Operations Research, Dr. Manu Madan took me under his wing. In one of his classes, he discussed two business concepts.

He taught me that the most successful companies or people with a sustainable business system follow this simple formula for success.

Figure out what the market's "Order Qualifying Criteria" is and gain a minimum competency for that requirement. And to excel in your niche market place, figure out what your "Order Winning Criteria" is and dominate it.

At the time of this writing (20+ years later), we still stay in touch and visit. I am always mindful of what I learned from Dr. Madan, and am grateful for his energy, effort, and encouragement to teach me to always be a student of the market.

"I was built for Comfort, Not Speed" by Jim Licata

Jim Licata is a good friend, fellow investor, and business partner. Funny thing about Jim and I is that, over the course of our relationship to-date, we have only met twice in person. Regardless, we have candid dialogues, freely exchange ideas, and constantly discuss reframing problems as hidden opportunities. I feel like I have known Jim for a lifetime and, whenever we pick up the phone to chat, it seems just like chatting with an old friend.

I'd like to share a discussion topic that Jim and I have been talking about on and off for over a year. I believe Jim has cracked the code for managing Multiple Streams of Income.

Multiple Streams of Income:

This is a topic that we have been discussing and kicking

about for a while. It always sounds so good to have multiple streams of income coming in. However, the limiting factor always comes down to having enough time and energy to do a good job managing the work from multiple streams of projects or deals.

Over, and through a year of dialog discussing multiple projects we worked on together and independently, Jim came up with the greatest jewel of wisdom. He figured out how he could manage multiple streams of income producing projects by doing the same thing. Be the "Money" guy.

For all the projects Jim is involved in, he always parks himself as the Banker, or Money Guy. Then he lets his team do the rest of the work. Finding deals, doing due diligence, managing the property, etc.

So now, Jim gets to cherry pick and get involved in select projects with people he likes and trusts. Jim just does more of the same thing. And as he does more and more of the same thing, he gets better and better at it. Today, he is a respected authority, resource, and go-to person on the subject of being the "MONEY" guy.

Jim spent some quality time to carefully define his preferred place in the Real Estate game, and he is accomplishing more by doing less.

Quotes

- "Worry does not empty tomorrow of its sorrow. It empties today of its strength." Corrie Ten Boom

- "Alone we can do so little; together we can do so much." Helen Keller

- "Find your place on the food chain, and DOMINATE it." William Teh

Summary:

- Figure out your ONE thing, and DOMINATE it.

Chapter 9: Happy Choices 5 Minute Review

1. What are your 3 main takeaways?

    i_____

    ii_____

    iii_____

2. Are you Happy with your present Situation?   YES/NO

3. If YES: What are the 3 things you can do more to improve?

    i_____

    ii_____

    iii_____

4. If NO: Reflect on 3 things that you are unhappy with:

    i_____

    ii_____

    iii_____

5. What are 3 things you can unlearn to be less unhappy/more Happy?

    i_____

    ii_____

    iii_____

Chapter 10
Choose to Fulfill your Desires
or Be Happy

I believe that satisfying our desires is not the same as seeking happiness.

In his audio book, "How to Succeed in Business and in Life," Dr. Nido Qubein shares how he observes that a person's lifestyle can be broadly categorized into 1 of 4 buckets.

Let's consider Dr. Nido Qubein's "Lifestyle" choices, and my take on it...

Activity-Centered Lifestyle
People with an Activity-centered lifestyle are always busy.

"We can maintain our activities as long as we have our health."

Possession-Centered Lifestyle
People with a Possession-Centered lifestyle are more interested in collecting stuff than using it, and may one day find out that, having this stuff does not really bring one happiness.

"When we place a higher value on possessions than on relationships, perhaps one day too late, we may discover that our misplaced priorities may have caused us to miss out on creating more memorable experiences with people we love and care about."

Relationship-Centered Lifestyle
People with a Relationship-Centered Lifestyle care about maintaining relationships, and may be afraid to be truthful, honest, and open with their feelings."

"We may sometimes compromise our own happiness just to maintain, or preserve the relationship."

Principled-Centered Lifestyle
People with Principled-Centered Lifestyles believe that they should live their life according to their values or beliefs.

"When we are too rigid with our values and beliefs, we may find that that we can be "right" and "alone."

Tying it up with a Single Question

May I suggest a single ribbon to tie our lifestyle together with this simple question? I believe that there are no right or wrong answers. The more quickly we discover this, the more quickly we can make better choices for ourselves.

"What is the purpose of life?"

Having a clear or single purpose for our life, we can better focus our energies towards managing our activities, possessions, and relationships to bring us closer to achieving our purpose.

We may get a slightly different perspective on life when we start losing our health, lose a loved one, or one day wake up and realize that there are fewer days left on the calendar to live than days lived.

When we find out that there is less sand left on the top of the hourglass of life than at the bottom, perhaps we will begin to place a higher value on our remaining time, and what, where, and whom to spend it with.

> *"Why wait for the inevitable future to arrive,*
> *and then show up unprepared,*
> *or worse yet don't show up."*

I'd like to share this simple, lovely, and touching story of "The Giving Tree" with you.

The Giving Tree
By Shel Silverstein

Once there was a tree. And she loved a little boy. And every day the boy would come. And he would gather her leaves. And make them into crowns and play king of the forest

He would climb up her trunk. And swing from her branches.

And when he was tired he would sleep in her shade.

And the boy loved the tree Very much . . . and the tree was happy.

But time went by, and the boy grew older. And the tree was often alone. Then one day the boy came to the tree and the tree said:

"Come, Boy, come and climb up my trunk and swing from my branches and eat apples and play in my shade and be "happy".

"I am too big to climb and play," said the boy. "I want to buy things and have fun. I want some money.

Can you give me some money?"

"I'm sorry," said the tree, "but I have no money.
I have only leaves and apples. Take my apples, Boy, and sell them in the city. Then you will have money and you'll be happy".

And so the boy climbed up the tree and gathered her apples and carried them away. And the tree was happy . . .

But the boy stayed away for a long time and the tree was sad.

And then one day the boy came back and the tree shook with joy, and she said:

"Come, Boy come and climb up my trunk and swing from my branches and eat apples and play in my shade and be "happy"...

"I am too busy to climb trees," said the boy. "I want a house to keep me warm," he said. "I want a wife and I want children, and so I need a house. Can you give me a house?"

"I have no house" said the tree. The forest is my house, said the tree "but you may cut off my branches and build a house. Then you will be happy."

And so the boy cut off her branches and carried them away to build a house. And the tree was happy.

But the boy stayed away for a long time and the tree was sad. And when he came back, the tree was so happy she could hardly speak.

"Come, Boy" she whispered, "Come and play"

"I am too old and sad to play." said the boy. "I want a boat that will take me away from here. Can you give me a boat?"

"Cut down my trunk and make a boat," said the tree. "Then you can sail away and be happy."

And so the boy cut down her trunk and made a boat and sailed away.

And the tree was happy . . . but not really.

And after a long time the boy came back again.

"I am sorry, Boy, "said the tree, "but I have nothing left to give you — my apples are gone."

"My teeth are too weak for apples", said the boy.

"My branches are gone," said the tree. "You cannot swing on them — "

"I am too old to swing on branches," said the boy.

"My trunk is gone," said the tree. "You cannot climb — "

"I am too tired to climb," said the boy.

"I am sorry" sighed the tree. "I wish that I could give you something. . . but I have nothing left. I am just an old stump. I am sorry..."

"I don't need very much now" said the boy. "Just a quiet place to sit and rest. I am very tired"

"Well," said the tree, straightening herself up as much as she could, "an old stump is good for sitting and resting. Come, Boy, sit down... and rest."

And the boy did.

And the tree was happy...

Quotes:

- "There is only one happiness in this life, to love and be loved." George Sand

- "Be happy today, by preparing to be happy tomorrow." William Teh

- "Happiness begins with the letting go of desires." William Teh

- "The more you hide your feelings, the more they show. The more you deny your feelings, the more they grow." Unknown

- "Genius might be the ability to say a profound thing in a simple way." Charles Bukowski

Summary:

- Choose Happiness as a destination or Journey.

- Satisfying desires may not be the same as being happy

- What is the purpose of life?

Chapter 10: Happy Choices 5 Minute Review

1. What are your 3 main takeaways?

    i_____

    ii_____

    iii_____

2. Are you Happy with your present Situation?   YES/NO

3. If YES: What are the 3 things you can do more to improve?

    i_____

    ii_____

    iii_____

4. If NO: Reflect on 3 things that you are unhappy with:

    i_____

    ii_____

    iii_____

5. What are 3 things you can unlearn to be less unhappy/more Happy?

    i_____

    ii_____

    iii_____

Chapter 11
Choose to Graciously Accept
or Courageously Press On

January 18, 2014, I received a Facebook message from my cousin Daniel. "Hey, I thought you would want to know, my dad has just been diagnosed with late stage liver cancer."

My cousin Daniel is a self-made entrepreneur. After graduating from the prestigious National University of Singapore, Daniel started his own company called Web Puppies, an online agency based in Singapore helping companies build creative and user-friendly solutions for Internet marketing and web design. Today, 14 years later, he is the Managing Director of the company, managing over a dozen or so prestigious name brand web sites.

"Oh dear!!! What is the impact of the diagnosis?" I messaged back.

"3-6 months left." Daniel messaged back. "OMG . . . That is crazy!" I replied. "How is Uncle Johnny feeling? What made him go find out?" I asked.

"We are speaking to more doctors to look for alternatives. Pain and loss of appetite. We are all still struggling to accept, you can call him now if you want, he is at home." Daniel messaged back.

"Hope Aunty Jannie (Daniel's mother), Leon (his brother), you, and your children are coping OK with this shocking news. I am at a loss for words . . ." I messaged back.

"Thanks . . . think my dad would like to hear from you." Daniel messaged back.

"Yes. I am very close to your father. He is a HUGE encouragement to me." I messaged back.

"Nod" messaged Daniel. "I hope so too, days are so precious now."

"Yes Sir. Thanks so much for letting me know. I really appreciate your reaching out to me." I messaged back.

The next day, Sunday evening here in Austin, Texas, I called Uncle Johnny on his cell phone. Singapore is 14 hours ahead, so it was about 10:00a.m. on Monday.

My Uncle was at the CPF (Central Provident Fund) building getting ready to settle his assets and affairs. The Central Provident Fund is Singapore's comprehensive social security savings plan for retirement, paying for your home, and providing sufficient savings to meet your medical needs in your old age.

We chatted for a bit while my Uncle and Aunty were queuing in line to get service from an agent at the counter. I asked him what made him go see a doctor to find out what was going with him. He told me that he had been losing his appetite, losing a lot of weight, and was feeling much weaker.

Aunty Jannie, Leon and Daniel kept telling him to go get a check-up from a doctor. A couple of blood and other tests later, the doctors told him that he had late stage liver cancer. It would have taken approximately 2 years for the cancer to advance to such a stage. It was a very rough weekend for my Uncle, Aunty, and cousins. By Sunday night, my Uncle Johnny graciously accepted the hand of cards he was dealt, and made it a point first thing on Monday morning to go settle his affairs so that Aunty Jannie, Leon, and Daniel would be properly provided for.

My Uncle Johnny was glad that he did not find out about his cancer, as the last couple of years were some of the happiest times of his life, taking care, and spending time with his grandchildren.

"Not knowing that I had cancer, I lived my life fully without worry."

"When I found out I had cancer and the doctors told me that I had less than 6 months to live, suddenly so many things became unimportant."

Fast-forward February 17, 2014
"Good morning." I messaged Daniel. "How is Uncle Johnny's condition?"

"Hi, he (my dad) is recovering well. They managed to get out 99% of the cancer and will be doing preventive chemotherapy on him. After the doctor opened him up, said he had at most 3-6 months and it was very fortunate that we operated when we did. Now he should have years left at least." Daniel messaged back on Facebook.

"Wow, that is AMAZING and AWESOME news! You are the best, I heard that you NEVER gave up and found the best doctors to take care of your father!" I Facebook messaged back.

"Oh hey, where did you hear that from? Yeah, it was quite hard when so many doctors tell you it is hopeless". Daniel messaged back.

"Your father said you never gave up on him regardless of what the other useless doctors said!" I messaged back to Daniel.

Fast-forward to March 1, 2014
"He (dad) is recovering well. (He) can walk around and drive already. He needs to get better before he is able to start chemotherapy. Doctors estimate 2 weeks more. On the whole, the treatments have been incredibly successful. Doctors have even commented that it is bordering on divine intervention." Facebook message from Daniel to me.

At the time of this writing (May, 2014) my Uncle Johnny is doing well. His stamina is back, his breath strong, and Aunty Jannie and he are both enjoying taking care of their grand children, getting them ready for school, and spending time with them.

There is a beautiful nursery rhyme by Mother Goose that so beautifully describes the peace of mind, which my Uncle had when he discovered he had cancer, and the never-give-up attitude his children Daniel and Leon had for their parents.

> *For every ailment under the sun,*
> *There is a remedy or there is none;*
> *If there be one, try to find it;*
> *If there is none, never mind it.*

I believe that when our purpose or priority in life becomes clearer, everything will start to fall in place, or away.

I'd like to conclude this chapter by sharing "The Serenity Prayer" drafted by the American theologian Reinhold Niebuhr (1892-1971).

The best known version of "The Serenity Prayer" is:

God, grant me the serenity to accept
the things I cannot change,
The courage to change the things I can,
And the wisdom to know the difference.

Quotes:

- "The days are so precious now." Daniel Tay

- "Not knowing that I had cancer, I lived my life fully without worry." Johnny Tay

- "Suddenly, a lot of things are not important to me anymore." Johnny Tay

Summary:

- Find peace with your decisions

Chapter 11: Happy Choices 5 Minute Review

1. What are your 3 main takeaways?

    i_____

    ii_____

    iii_____

2. Are you Happy with your present Situation?   YES/NO

3. If YES: What are the 3 things you can do more to improve?

    i_____

    ii_____

    iii_____

4. If NO: Reflect on 3 things that you are unhappy with:

    i_____

    ii_____

    iii_____

5. What are 3 things you can unlearn to be less unhappy/more Happy?

    i_____

    ii_____

    iii_____

Chapter 12
Choose to Make Happy Choices

I believe we cannot make happy choices when we are Mad, Scared, or Confused.

Being Mad or Scared
When we are Mad or Scared, we are most probably in a highly non-positive, emotionally stressed state. Now is when our Fight or Flight instincts take over making decisions. We are making decisions to "survive" and not to be "happy".

Being Confused
I believe Confusion is the main cause for unnecessary worry. The simplest definition of confusion is "unable to think clearly." Being confused is not the same as being uncertain, or having a problem.

Being uncertain can be remedied, with finding out more information.

Here are some of my thoughts about having a problem.

>*What is the definition of a Problem?*
>*Every problem has a solution.*

>*What is the solution for every problem?*
>*Ask the right person the right questions.*

What do you call a problem without a solution?
A complaint.

Worry is the main reason for unhealthy stress. When we worry, so many things we worry about never really come true. Have you heard the phrase "worry wart"? A "worry wart" is a person who tends to dwell unduly on difficulty or troubles. Most of which never happen.

Take away:
> Confusion => Worry => Unhealthy Stress => Make Poor Choices

I believe there are at least 3 ways we can learn to make better choices.

Learn from our own experiences
Unfortunately, learning this way may rob years of happiness from our lives. We may have to stumble upon an experience to realize that we have missed out on life, or worse yet, not have an experience to realize what we have missed out on.

Take away: We don't know what we don't know.

Learn from others' experiences
This can greatly shorten our learning curve. Unfortunately, learning this way may also be a hit

and miss strategy depending with whom we spend time, and if we find their experiences are relevant to us.

Take away: We know what we don't know by learning from someone else.

Get help, or coaching
Learning this way can help accelerate our progress to happiness by having someone lead, show, and guide us.

Take away: We learn from someone who knows what we don't know.

From my personal experiences, and observations, I'd like to share with you the 3 shackles of unhappiness and 3 secrets of happiness. These secrets are elusively hidden in our everyday life, activities, and people we spend time with.

The 3 shackles of unhappiness are:
Limiting Beliefs
Misplaced Priorities
Unproductive Relationships

The 3 keys to happiness are:
Liberating Beliefs
Clear Purpose
Healthy relationships

As we wind down to the end of the book, I'd like to share a scene from the movie, "The Bucket List" with you.

In this movie, two terminally ill men escape from a cancer ward and head off on a road trip with a wish of to-do's before they die.

Morgan Freeman plays Carter Chambers a working class mechanic. Carter is an intellectual mechanic who spent 45 years greased up under the hood of a car so that his children would have the kind of life he'd always dreamed about for himself.

Jack Nicholson plays Edward Cole a corporate billionaire. Edward is debaucherous, lascivious and personally over-indulgent while always keeping an eye wide open for his self interest. If he had a legacy, it would be his vast business empire.

In the scene where they are overlooking the Egyptian pyramids, Freeman explains to Nicholson that when souls got to the entrance of heaven, the gods asked them two questions. Their answers determined if they would be admitted into heaven or not.

The two questions were . . .

"Have you found joy in your life?

"Has your life brought joy to others?"

These two simple questions bring a refreshingly new perspective on the purpose of life for me.

If I understand the Egyptians gods correctly, being right or wrong does not get us into heaven.

Be Happy

I enjoyed sharing these dozen chapters together with you. Making happy choices is simple but not necessarily easy. The clearer we are about our purpose, the simpler are our choices. We can live a happier life simply by the choices we make, choosing the right people to spend time with, and picking the right environment to thrive in.

My name is William Teh. I am a husband, father, and a life investor. I invite you to Reflect, Unlearn, and Live Better by making happier choices.

Quotes:

- "People make bad choices if they're mad or scared or stressed." Lyrics from song "Fixer Upper" in the movie "Frozen"

- "We hold these truths to be self-evident; that all men are created equal; that they are endowed by their creator with certain unalienable rights; that among these are life, liberty, and the pursuit of happiness" Thomas Jefferson

- "However many holy words you read, however many you speak, what good will they do you if you do not act upon them?" Buddha

- "What is the difference between Life and Death? It is when time becomes eternity." William Teh

Summary:

- Live Better by Making Happy Choices.

Chapter 12: Happy Choices 5 Minute Review

1. What are your 3 main takeaways?

    i_____

    ii_____

    iii_____

2. Are you Happy with your present Situation?   YES/NO

3. If YES: What are the 3 things you can do more to improve?

    i_____

    ii_____

    iii_____

4. If NO: Reflect on 3 things that you are unhappy with:

    i_____

    ii_____

    iii_____

5. What are 3 things you can unlearn to be less unhappy/more Happy?

    i_____

    ii_____

    iii_____

To Order:

"Make Happy Choices"

Use this order form or go to *www.highhopespublishing.com*
Bulk copies: call High Hopes Publishing at 1-888-742-0074.

Please send _____ copies to:

_____
Name

_____
Address

_____
City/State/Zip/Phone

Method of payment: (check one)

Check _____   Credit Card _____

Credit card information: _____
                         Card number

                         _____
                         Expiration   3 digit code from card back

                         _____
                         Name on card (if different from above)
                         (Books will be sent to the address above)

                         _____
                         Signature

# of books ordered _____ x $24.95/per book = $ _____
Note: Shipping/handling will be added to your order

Mail this order form to: or FAX to:
     High Hopes Publishing   1-512-868-0548
     1618 Williams Drive #5
     Georgetown, TX 78628

A Note From the Publisher...

Once again, we are honored to publish another book for William Teh. I have come to discover and appreciate, from numerous breakfasts and telephone conversations with William that he lives in a "less is more" world. This makes him a contrarian to how most people think and behave. My revelation is that William is right.

When you look at the chapter headings of this book, you can discern William's message for you: you have a choice in everything that affects your happiness. Many of us tend to believe that we are pre-destined to behave or react a certain way based on our heredity, environment or what the cat did on the carpet. You will find that William's gentle writing style taps you on the shoulder and offers you refreshing new options.

As William's publisher and editor, one of my jobs has been to comb through his text and prepare it for print. As I have been doing that, I have found what I hope you do too . . . a feast masquerading as a snack! The page count, the chapter length, and even the type face may appear to make this book seem light but do not be fooled. Less IS more.

You will discover succulent morsels within these pages to help you reframe your thoughts. Read the book cover-to-cover to cultivate a taste for the 12-course gourmet meal provided. Then, re-read any chapter choice that you like so you can focus and savor the flavor like a desert.

My copy of *"Make Happy Choices"* resides next to William's earlier book *"13 Ways to Accomplish More by Doing Less"*. They will both live next to my desk and never collect dust. This is one of my Happy Choices.

Eugene Vasconi, President, High Hopes Publishing

CPSIA information can be obtained at www.ICGtesting.com
Printed in the USA
LVOW10*0034200914

405013LV00002B/5/P